Show Me Your Ways, O Lord

Devotions on the Psalms of Advent

Kathryn Nishibayashi, Beth-Sarah Wright,
Nancy Frausto, and Kim Fox

Library of Congress Cataloging-in-Publication Data

Names: Nishibayashi, Kathryn, author.

Title: Show me your ways, o Lord : devotions on the Psalms of Advent/ Kathryn Nishibayashi [and three others].

Description: Cincinnati, Ohio : Forward Movement, [2024] | Summary: "Bless your Advent journey with these inspiring daily devotions exploring psalms from the season. Join four noted authors as they offer diverse perspectives on psalms of adoration, lament, repentance, and thanks. This collection connects us to the eternal truths of scripture by reflecting on the assigned Sunday psalms for Advent from all three liturgical years. Each daily devotion includes prompts for going deeper with personal reflection or faithful practices. During a time of chaos and confusion, these daily devotions help you stay anchored in the knowledge that "The earth is the Lord's and all that is in it, the world and all who dwell therein" (Psalm 24:1)"-- Provided by publisher.

Identifiers: LCCN 2024011653 (print) | LCCN 2024011654 (ebook) | ISBN 9780880285247 | ISBN 9780880285247 (ebook)

Subjects: LCSH: Advent--Prayers and devotions. | Bible. Psalms-- Devotional literature. | BISAC: RELIGION / Holidays / Christmas & Advent | RELIGION / Christianity / Episcopalian

Classification: LCC BV40 .N555 2024 (print) | LCC BV40 (ebook) | DDC 242/.332--dc23/eng/20240516

LC record available at https://lccn.loc.gov/2024011653

LC ebook record available at https://lccn.loc.gov/2024011654

Cover art: *Windswept Majesty* by Claudia Smith. Learn more about Claudia in the About the Artist page in the back of the book.

Psalm quotations are from the Book of Common Prayer.

inspire disciples.empower evangelists.

All rights reserved worldwide.

#2681 | ISBN: 978-0-88028-524-7

© 2024 Forward Movement

Show Me Your Ways, O Lord

Devotions on the Psalms of Advent

Kathryn Nishibayashi, Beth-Sarah Wright,
Nancy Frausto, and Kim Fox

FORWARD MOVEMENT
Cincinnati, Ohio

Show Me Your Ways, O Lord

Devotions on the Psalms of Advent

Contents

Introduction ix

Week One 1

Week Two 23

Week Three 43

Week Four 65

Appendix—Psalms 87

About the Authors 103

About the Artist 109

About Forward Movement 111

INTRODUCTION

There's a reason why we have favorite songs. With just a few words, they jettison us back to a treasured memory: a lullaby from grandma, a carefree drive on a summer day with friends, a first dance with a partner. Songs are faithful companions, putting words to emotions—from joy and delight to grief and sorrow.

So it is with the psalms. These ancient Hebrew hymns express praise and thanksgiving as well as anger and lament. Through the grace of God, we have the gift of 150 psalms that meet us where we are, grappling with a range of emotions, and invite us to go where we should: into the embrace of a God who loves us in good times and bad.

This Advent, we turn to the psalms with a petition: "Show me your ways, O Lord." Show me how to forgive when wounded. Show me how to love without condition. Show me how to praise you, how to offer thanksgiving, and how to be faithful in times of uncertainty. Show me, O Lord, the ways to prepare my heart to welcome your son.

We asked four faithful women, noted leaders across the church, to guide us through the psalms during the season of Advent. They selected excerpts from the psalms appointed on the Sundays of each week, and they offer stories and wisdom—and a partner for the journey. Perhaps you'll discover a favorite psalm, just as you have a favorite song, one that will offer promise and solace each time you hear it. One that shows you the way to God's abiding love.

Richelle Thompson
Editor

Of note: *We included a full four weeks of meditations for Advent. But the number of days in the season of Advent depends on the calendar. Feel free to skip ahead to Christmas Eve and Christmas Day (and, if you'd like, read the days you missed during the fourth week of Advent, too!). In the Appendix, you can find the full readings of the psalms cited in the meditations.*

Show Me Your Ways, O Lord

The First Week of Advent

Sunday

I was glad when they said to me, "Let us go to the house of the LORD." Now our feet are standing within your gates, O Jerusalem.

PSALM 122:1-2

Think about the last time you went on a trip. Think about the preparations that you had to make before the trip began. They might have included organizing house or pet sitters, booking hotels or rental cars, and planning the itinerary for your time away. Unless it was a completely spontaneous trip, you likely needed some time to complete the necessary preparations. Think about the actual trip and the feelings you had as the journey to the destination began and the excitement began to build. Now think about the arrival at your destination. Whether you had travel challenges or not, you probably experienced relief and excitement when you arrived. The adventure could begin!

If I were to put these psalm verses in a modern-day context, I imagine the psalmist saying something like, "It made me happy when my friends invited me on a trip. Now we've made it to our vacation spot, and I'm ready to have fun."

I love reading this psalm as we begin Advent and our journey toward Jesus's birth. The words set the context for this season. In this first week, we hear the invitation, "Let us go to the house of the LORD." As I prepare my heart for the manger, I think about the first nativity story: the journey Mary and Joseph took, the preparations they had to make in anticipation of the birth, the challenges they had in finding a place to rest on their journey, and the celebration upon Jesus's birth.

We don't hear about whether Mary or Joseph made this journey alone, but I imagine many traveled together to fulfill the census demands of Emperor Augustus. I imagine the stories they shared over campfires at night or as they made the long trek on foot from Nazareth to Bethlehem. In my journeys, I have found my time deeply enriched by friends and family—and by those I have met along the way.

This is just the first day of the first week of our preparations for Advent. As you begin your preparations, take time to be intentional about your actions. Think about what the preparations mean to you. Think about how they relate to the first Christmas. And don't take this journey alone. Join with your faith community in sharing the hopes, anticipation, and excitement of Advent and Christmas. In a season where it is easy to rush through things and check off the proverbial boxes, take the time to soak it all in and savor the memories you are making or helping to create for others during this season.

Going Deeper

What one way will you be intentional about preparing your heart during Advent? You might consider a commitment to reading from the psalms every day.

A full list of the Advent psalms can be found at the back of this book.

This Week's Author

Kathryn Nishibayashi is the fourth generation of her family to be a member at St. Mary's Episcopal Church in Los Angeles, a church founded for Japanese immigrants but now home to a multicultural congregation. She received her master of divinity degree from Church Divinity School of the Pacific in 2023 and is in discernment for Holy Orders.

Monday

Restore us, O God of hosts; show the light of your countenance, and we shall be saved.

PSALM 80:3,7,18

As a former elementary school teacher, I know that repetition is key to incorporating a phrase or action more fully into your body, mind, and spirit. Conventional wisdom says you must do something 21 times before it becomes a habit. Whether we need 21 times or not, the more often a phrase is heard, the more likely it is that we will remember it in the future.

Scattered throughout the Bible are verses that are repeated, sometimes verbatim, others repeated with slight differences. In Psalm 80, the phrase "Restore us, O God of hosts; show the light of your countenance, and we shall be saved" is repeated three times. Perhaps the psalmist chose to repeat the phrase to grab the worshipper's attention.

Meditation practitioners often repeat a mantra or phrase throughout their practice. As the phrase repeats, it sinks into one's bones. While this can be powerful, there's also the possibility that it can backfire. Sometimes, when something is repeated so often, it can feel like it loses meaning. In our tradition, we follow a liturgical calendar, which means we visit the same liturgical seasons in the same order year after year. We have a schedule of readings that changes every two or three years, but the overarching themes remain. Further, our Sunday liturgies repeat the same words and prayers week after week. With such repetition, it can be easy to get complacent and forget to focus on the meaning of the words we pray. This has happened to me occasionally throughout the years.

But once I am aware that the prayers have become rote, I work to adopt a new intention and awareness so I can renew my focus on the words of the prayers, even the most familiar ones. While the New Revised Standard Version of the Bible begins this verse with the words, "Restore us," the King James version of the Bible says, "Turn us again." As we turn again to the season of Advent, we begin a new liturgical year. Much like January 1 serves as the beginning of the secular new year, Advent serves as a time to reflect and reset our hopes and expectations for the coming

Show Me Your Ways, O Lord

season and the coming year. With each new year, we have the chance to begin again. We can look forward in hope to the possibilities and opportunities that lie ahead.

Going Deeper

Perhaps in this season of Advent, you might find a word to latch onto as a mantra for the season. This repetition might be a helpful anchor in a busy time or provide an opportunity for deeper reflection. What word might you take on as a mantra for Advent? What might you do to make the anticipation of this season a fresh experience or take on a new or different meaning for you?

Tuesday

You have fed them with the bread of tears;
you have given them bowls of tears to drink.

At an adult education forum at a church on the first
Sunday of Advent, a facilitator asked participants
to share their earliest memories of Advent. Having
grown up in the church, I couldn't remember how I
learned about the meaning of Advent, but it seems
like I understood from an early age that Advent was a
time of preparation for Christmas.

Of course, in the secular world, the preparations for
Christmas often have little to do with church or Bible
study and more to do with buying and wrapping
presents, baking treats for family and friends, wearing
cozy pajamas while sipping festive beverages, and
more. This is sometimes what children (and some
adults) think of when preparing for Christmas.

Recently, I was listening to a local radio station
that had switched from its regular music playlists

to Christmas music, starting on Thanksgiving Day. They mentioned how Christmas music makes people happy and nostalgic with memories. I do think that hearing the same music year after year elicits some nostalgia as people remember Christmases past. But, as I have gotten older, I have become more aware of the challenges this supposed-to-be-joyous season can bring, especially for people who are grieving.

Some churches respond to this pain with a "Blue Christmas" service, usually offered in the week or so leading up to December 25. As one church explains, not everyone finds comfort and joy in the bright lights and sparkles of the season; the Blue Christmas service offers a space for contemplation and reflection so participants can grapple with the complex emotions that this season may bring.

When I assisted at a Blue Christmas service, people came with a variety of needs on their hearts, including prayers of hope that their family would come together to celebrate the holiday in a civil manner, prayers for stamina that they could maintain the energy to keep up with all the demands on their time, and prayers that they would be accepted for living their authentic truth at their family's gathering. It was in praying with and for these people that I truly realized what a complicated time this season can be, and I am grateful for churches that offer spaces for people to deal with their emotions in a sacred space. Sometimes, it is only after processing the grief (whether the loss of a family member, the changing of a beloved tradition, or any kind of loss) that there is a space for hope to break through. Perhaps the Blue Christmas attendees leave the service with a sense of hope that God will remain with them through the challenging holiday, making it just a little easier for them to move forward.

Going Deeper

In this first week of Advent, where we focus on hope, what are you hoping for? What might you need to let go of and leave behind to prepare yourself for the coming Christmas celebration?

Wednesday

Let none who look to you be put to shame; let the
treacherous be disappointed in their schemes.

PSALM 25:2

Whenever I engage in Bible study, whether to
prepare to preach or just out of my own curiosity,
I explore a variety of translations. It's a good practice
not to rely on only one version of any given Bible
passage.

I often find an interesting perspective in the Common
English Bible, a translation published in 2011
and sponsored by an alliance of several Protestant
denominations including the Episcopal Church.
For today's psalm, the Common English Bible says,
"Don't let anyone who hopes in you be put to shame."
The replacement of "look" with "hope" is compelling.
We are called to look for signs of hope in the Advent
season and beyond. I've heard it said that love is an
action word, but hope is too. We must take action to
seek out the hope: in the world, in another person, in
any given situation.

In this season of Advent, our hope is placed in the birth of a newborn baby. While I don't have any children of my own, I have spent much of my life with children: as a babysitter, camp counselor, teacher, sister, and more recently, an aunt. The birth of a new baby is filled with so much hope: hope for what they will become as they grow older, hope for the impact they will have on the world and people around them, and hope that the world will provide them what they need for a good life. And children are often beacons of hope for adults. Largely unaffected by the same stresses and challenges experienced by adults, children have a unique view of the world around them. Perhaps that's why Christmas pageants are such common occurrences in the Advent season: the telling of a story we adults know so well is infused with the energy and hope of children still finding their way in the world.

As followers of Jesus, we know that no other baby born thus far has had the same impact on the world as Jesus. God sent Jesus as Emmanuel, or God-with-us, to earth to remind us that God is always with us and that we must continue to seek out the hope that Jesus's birth brought to this world.

Going deeper

A common theme for the first week of Advent is hope. Think of the children in your life. What lessons of hope do they teach you? How can you look for hope—and act in hope?

Thursday

Show me your ways, O LORD, and teach me your paths. Lead me in your truth and teach me, for you are the God of my salvation; in you have I trusted all the day long.

PSALM 25:3-4

While Christmas is clearly a Christian holiday, it seems to have become co-opted by the secular world. The "Christmas creep" in retail stores seems to get earlier and earlier each year, with Christmas items appearing in stores sometimes as early as August or September. People who do not attend church regularly celebrate Christmas as a time to be with family and friends, give gifts, adorn their houses with festive decorations, and buy and decorate a Christmas tree. With all the consumerism that loudly surrounds the Christmas season, it can be easy to lose sight of the true meaning of Christmas. In response, you may have heard two common phrases in the lead-up to Christmas: "Jesus is the reason for the season" and "Keep Christ in Christmas." Even though I usually hear these phrases in more evangelical circles, there is a great deal of truth to them. We wouldn't have a Christmas holiday if it weren't for the birth of Jesus Christ. The birth of Jesus truly is the reason to celebrate. And the word Christmas derives from "Christ mass."

Advent is a time of preparation, and the readings we hear in church prepare and remind us of the true "reason for the season." Going to church during Advent is almost countercultural to the larger society. But by attending to our spiritual lives in the midst of the frenetic busyness of secular Christmas preparations, we can return to Christ as the anchor and touchstone of our faith. If we turn our lives and attention to Christ, we can, as these verses of Psalm 25 tell us, learn from the truth that God teaches us through the person of Jesus. We can turn to God when we need somewhere to place our trust. The Common English Bible translation says, "I put my hope in you" instead of "in you have I trusted."

With all the demands and pressures on our lives throughout the year and especially during the busy holiday time, we must remember to place our hope and trust in God that all things will work out to the glory of God. It might not always be in the timeframe we desire or show up in our lives in the way we want or expect, but we must remember that God can do infinitely more than we can ask or imagine (Ephesians 3:20), and that in itself is a reason to have hope during this season and beyond.

Going deeper

Commit to attending church at least once a week this Advent season. Your congregation may have other opportunities for worship and formation as well. Afford those invitations the same (or more) consideration as you do holiday parties and functions.

Friday

He guides the humble in doing right and teaches his way to the lowly. All the paths of the LORD are love and faithfulness to those who keep his covenant and his testimonies.

PSALM 25:8-9

I have a wide variety of T-shirts with various church-related sayings or images. In thinking about my collection, I realized that I have many shirts with quotes from Episcopal Presiding Bishop Michael B. Curry. Bishop Curry became known as "the love bishop" shortly after he preached at the royal wedding of Prince Harry and Meghan Markle in 2018. He frequently talks about love in his sermons and even wrote a book titled *Love is the Way* and was a featured subject in the documentary film *A Case for Love.* One of my favorite quotes of his says: "If it's not about love, it's not about God"—and yes, I do have that on a T-shirt!

God is love. And God's love was made incarnate in the person of Jesus whose birth we prepare for during

Advent. Anglican writer Christina Rossetti articulated this miracle in her poem "Love Came Down at Christmas." A now-common Christmas carol, the poem includes the phrase "love incarnate, love divine." What a wonderful summation of the baby Jesus, who was both fully human and fully divine! As Jesus grew older, he spread that love and hope to all the people he encountered, especially those society considered "less than" or "lowly."

In the rite of baptism in the Episcopal Church, the liturgy includes a series of promises as part of the the Baptismal Covenant. It is the agreement that the candidate makes—or, if an infant, the candidate's sponsors make—with God about how they will pattern their life going forward. One of the questions in the baptismal liturgy asks if the candidate will "seek and serve Christ in all persons, loving your neighbor as yourself," and another inquires whether the candidate will "strive for justice and peace among all people, and respect the dignity of every human being." These questions aren't for the faint of heart. They are big asks. But they call the candidate to live and love just as Jesus did. We have his example as we set about fulfilling these promises. But the even more amazing thing is that we don't have to do this hard work alone. The response to each of these questions is "I will, with God's help."

Covenants can be renewed, and as baptized Episcopalians, when we witness other baptisms, we can renew our own baptismal vows. Having the chance to repeat vows—whether baptismal, marital, or ordination—offers the opportunity to remember why we said yes to the commitment in the first place. When we seek to live out these promises, this covenant, we become a part of the way of love, love incarnate, love divine.

Going deeper

Read the service for baptism in the Book of Common Prayer, *starting on page 298. If you could design a T-shirt with your favorite phrase of the Baptismal Covenant, what would it say?*

Saturday

Because of the house of the LORD our God, I will seek to do you good.

PSALM 122:9

I am a self-proclaimed grammar nerd, and I've always been fascinated by languages and linguistics. On this verse, I went down a grammar and biblical translation rabbit hole. Thanks to the internet, I can have multiple translations at my fingertips in a matter of seconds.

Some translations talk about "good" as wealth, prosperity, or well-being. Various versions talk about seeking, working, wishing, or praying for the "good." At least in English, "good" is one of those words that seems fairly simple. But what does "good" truly mean? When someone responds to the question "How was your day?" with the word, "Good," do you truly have a sense of what happened in their day? In researching the Hebrew word for "good," I discovered multiple definitions and multiple ways the word is used throughout the Hebrew scriptures. I suppose the same is true in the way we use the word in English.

Show Me Your Ways, O Lord

One of my favorite TV shows growing up was *Boy Meets World*. Decades later, I still remember the details of the final scene of the series finale. As the teacher wishes the students well at the end of the year, he leaves them with these words: "Believe in yourself. Dream. Try. Do good." While he never clarifies what he means by "do good," it's clear that he's encouraging them to do good things in the world for others.

No matter the translation of this verse from Psalm 122, there's a common understanding that the meaning is about seeking the good for someone else. This reminds me of the African concept of *ubuntu*, which loosely translates to "I am because you are." Our humanity is linked with everyone else's humanity. This is a helpful reminder in this Advent season. Many churches and other organizations conduct various outreach activities to help those with fewer resources. We can and should give from our abundance—and be intentional about finding ways to do good.

Going deeper

Where might you be able to "do good" this Advent season? How might you make it a yearlong commitment?

The Second Week of Advent

Sunday

Give the King your justice, O God,
and your righteousness to the King's son;
That he may rule your people righteously
and the poor with justice;
That the mountains may bring prosperity
to the people,
and the little hills bring righteousness.
He shall defend the needy among the people;
he shall rescue the poor and crush the oppressor.

PSALM 72:1-4

This beautiful prayer poem from the Book of Psalms shows us a pathway to God's hopes for us and how we are expected to navigate the world. God's way is to look at this world and then act through the machinery of justice—a complex system of heart, mind, and hand. While the psalm is a prayer for a new king, we all have the power and the possibility to be God's partners here on earth. This psalm invites us to take up the divine leadership activity of treating people righteously and the poor with justice.

But what is justice anyway? We may think of charity or handouts and donations for the poor as the only means to achieve justice. While these acts are necessary, I came across a definition of justice that is a broader understanding and, I think, much more helpful. Saint Bonaventure, a thirteenth-century Italian theologian and bishop, describes justice as "the returning to its original beauty that which has been deformed." By this definition, we are asked to restore the world's original beauty by righting wrongs, restoring balance, and weeding out acts of oppression wherever we can. Justice, then, is seeing the beauty and divinity in others, no matter what. The pursuit of justice reveals the world's imbalances while maintaining human dignity. Justice sees the oppressed and the oppressor through a restorative lens. We have deformed God's beauty through our acts of selfishness, blindness, and desire for power. But all hope is not lost. We can still work toward recreating God's beauty through everyday acts of justice and righteousness. And when we do, we experience God's peace that passes all understanding.

One of the most striking memories I have of my mother is when I was a child riding in the back of her car, and she came to a complete stop on the side of the road. I did not know why we stopped. But then I saw my mother take off her shoes, get out of the car, and hand them to an elderly woman who was walking on bare feet on the side of the road. The woman thanked my mother and said, "God bless you."

This was an extraordinary act but not a singular one for my mother. She taught my siblings and me to seek out and see not only the poor but also the injustices in the world and to act, to make a difference. We watched her commitment to restoring imbalances through her nursing, her work with organizations for the homeless, and even her elegant way of restoring dignity in interactions when someone felt wronged or was abusing their position of perceived power.

When we strive to return "to its original beauty that which has been deformed," we move through life with our hearts bent toward justice, our minds creating opportunities for justice, and our hands enacting justice wherever we can. May we all have the courage, the presence, and the commitment to restore God's beauty by acting with God's justice.

Going Deeper

Do you pray to God to reveal a pathway forward in life? This Advent, pray to God to help you discover this pathway—God's dream for our lives.

This Week's Author

Beth-Sarah Wright works nationwide, encouraging individuals, communities, and institutions to develop the capacity for change and transformation. Originally from Jamaica, she has lived and studied worldwide, from Edinburgh, Scotland to San Juan, Puerto Rico. She is married to Robert C. Wright, the Episcopal Bishop of Atlanta, and they are parents to 5 adult children.

Monday

*He shall live as long as the sun and moon
endure, from one generation to another.*

*He shall come down like rain upon the mown
field, like showers that water the earth.*

*In his time shall the righteous flourish;
there shall be abundance of peace till the moon
shall be no more.*

PSALM 72:5-8

I remember someone once told me that everything
I needed to know about God was in my backyard.
Undoubtedly, I have felt closest to God when
observing the awesome wonder of God's natural
creations and can see God's fingerprints in the majesty
of the Grand Canyon, the profound peace in the
glassy waters of Lake Geneva, the lush comfort in the
canopy of plant life in Jamaica's Fern Gully, or simply
the smell of rain on a summer's day.

It is no surprise, then, that the psalm uses nature to
describe the divinely inspired acts of the King—that

his life and legacy shall endure as long as the sun and the moon. He may pour out his heart like rain showers upon the field, nurturing the earth so that righteousness shall sprout up and flourish and peace shall be abundant until the moon is no more. But all this flourishing and abundance needs a climate of justice and righteousness. As we saw in the first verses of Psalm 72, God's soil is amplified with the fertilizer of intentional acts of defending the needy, rescuing the poor, and crushing the oppressor.

These are the types of actions that should endure, strengthening and guiding each generation to come. Yet, we struggle as humans to carry out these acts and let ourselves become distracted by power, greed, and selfishness. We see who we want to see and help who we want to help. But there is no room for that thinking in the psalm's paradigm of abundance. Raindrops that shower the earth are filled with grace and mercy, falling everywhere with no exceptions. In God's ecosystem, all feel the freshness of the showers that water the earth, and peace shall be abundant.

Going Deeper

In this Advent season, how can we emulate God's provision for the most vulnerable among us? Let us begin by blessing and providing for others and seeing how God's ecosystem flourishes with a climate of justice and love.

Tuesday

Blessed be the Lord GOD, the God of Israel,
who alone does wondrous deeds!

And blessed be his glorious Name for ever!
and may all the earth be filled with his glory.
Amen. Amen.

PSALM 72:18-19

The Advent season is a time of preparation directing our hearts and minds to the anniversary of Christ's birth at Christmas. It is a time of waiting for Christ's coming, advent, into our lives. Yes, we prepare. Yes, we look forward to Christ's coming again. But do we stop to praise God amid the waiting? Do we pause to celebrate all that we have, all that we are, and all that we will become because of Christ Jesus?

At the end of this prayer poem, the final two verses are words of praise and glory. They are a doxology! They punctuate this prayer with ultimate praise to the one from whom all blessings flow. While this psalm is a prayer for an earthly king, God alone does wondrous deeds and marvelous things. It is God alone who deserves all the glory and whose name is blessed forever. And it is God alone whose glory can fill the entire earth.

We often forget to praise God, quickly jumping to petitions for help, healing, and rescue—or intercessions on behalf of others for their needs and guidance. We may thank God for the blessings in our lives or make prayers of confession for the deeds we have left undone. We may even pray to give our lives to God to use us here on earth. But honoring God for being God often escapes us. Yet, this praise is the purpose of these final words of the psalm, lest we forget the source of it all.

Going Deeper

What would it look like if we used these days leading to Christ's coming to praise God intentionally? How would this change how we see our lives, how we see ourselves, and how we see each other?

Wednesday

You have been gracious to your land, O LORD,
you have restored the good fortune of Jacob.

You have forgiven the iniquity of your people
and blotted out all their sins.

PSALM 85:1-2

In these verses, I am most struck by the word
"restored." It is a word infused with hope, with the
knowledge that with God, we will be made whole
again—a state of being that is only possible with
God's mercy and grace.

I love the word "restored" because it means that
despite my failings, sins, and iniquities, God's
salvation is at hand. It is possible to be made new
again. Oh, how I yearned for that feeling when I felt
my most broken. In the depths of depression, it can
feel as if there is no possibility of being restored or put
back together. I know it felt that way for me. But, as
the words in this psalm remind us, God is gracious,
forgives iniquities, blots out sins, and makes people
new again. God is faithful.

Show Me Your Ways, O Lord

Advent is another opportunity for us to say yes again to God's faithfulness, to say yes, again, to God's ability to see our full stories—all of who we are, all of whom we have been, and all of who we will become and make us whole. In one of my books, I wrote "A Prayer for Our Stories." It is a prayer for us in this season to be reminded of the awesome power of God to make wonderful reversals in our stories, where new chapters are possible, and where God can always write the endings.

Going Deeper

Offer this prayer, "A Prayer for Our Stories," to God today.

Lord, I embrace my story; I embody my story; My story does not embody me. I seek the humility to listen more; I seek the courage to share more; All so I may magnify you more. I am free to become who I am; I am empowered to become who I am; I choose to become who I am. Tell me your story, I tell you my story. New stories. Renew stories. I knew my story. My new story. I have your story. Become your story. Be your story. Stories restore. Restore my story. Story restored. REPEAT.

Thursday

I will listen to what the LORD God is saying,
for he is speaking peace to his faithful people
and to those who turn their hearts to him.

Truly, his salvation is very near to those who
*   fear him,*
that his glory may dwell in our land.

PSALM 85:8-9

About 15 years ago, I experienced a period of great darkness in my life. I was gripped with a debilitating bout of depression where I could not pray or hear God's voice. My healing began with the divine convergence of a Bible study I happened to attend, when an angel squeezed into the body of a then-86-year-old woman and shared the powerful words of Romans 8:26-27: "Likewise the Spirit helps us in our weakness; for we do not know how to pray as we ought, but that very Spirit intercedes with sighs too deep for words. And God, who searches the heart, knows what is the mind of the Spirit, because the Spirit intercedes for the saints according to the will of God."

In many ways, those words saved my life, and I could feel the rush of peace washing over my body. For in that moment, I knew what God was saying. I just needed to listen. I needed to listen and be reminded that God is steadfast, always with me no matter the circumstance, and wants peace and abundant life.

When we turn our hearts to God, both in the moments of joy and suffering, we will hear God's voice. We only need to listen keenly to what God is saying. God's salvation, deliverance, and rescuing power are always near to us when we fear God. To be clear, to fear God is not to cower in God's presence; rather, to fear God is to be in utter awe. It is to revere God's omnipresence, power, and authority. It is to stand in awe of God's majesty, wisdom, justice, mercy, and divine timing!

At my lowest, I did not believe that God would hear my cries of sorrow. Self-limiting thoughts can do that. They can be loud and drown out God's voice. But when I heard those words from Romans, I remembered how awesome God is and that God would intervene even when I did not have the words. My prayers changed significantly after that moment, and I offer them in this season of Advent, where we await the awe-some birth of Christ.

Going Deeper

Say these words aloud—at prayer time, meals, and just before bed. Gracious and all-knowing God, in everything I do, in everything I am, in everything I will become, let my actions glorify you always!

Friday

Mercy and truth have met together;
righteousness and peace have kissed each other.

PSALM 85:10

Did you notice the powerful coming together of
four distinct features of God's promises in this verse?
Mercy, truth, righteousness, and peace. This divine
convergence is not only God's promise but also God's
invitation for us to live our lives. It is a road map. We
need only to follow it.

Can we exercise mercy while coming face to face with
truth in our daily lives? Can we uphold accountability
while being merciful to ourselves and others? Can
we live with righteousness and justice on our lips and
speak peace into existence simultaneously? This is our
hope. This is the foreshadowing of our world. This is
where we hope to be and who we hope to become.

Methodist theologian Timothy Tennent offers that
the coming together of these four key aspects of
God's promise occurs four times. The first time is

through the incarnation, when Jesus fully embodies righteousness and peace, the very incarnation of God's mercy and truth. The second time occurs on the cross, satisfying God's righteousness and peace with this world and God's ultimate expression of mercy and truth. The third time is in the mystery of the eucharist, or great thanksgiving, where the sacrament is the ongoing reminder of the sacrifice of Christ, which brings mercy, truth, righteousness, and peace all together. Tennent argues that the fourth time— when all these realities come together—still awaits us when Christ returns and will set all things right.

In Advent, we await the coming again of these four dimensions in Christ's birth. Yet we are given an opportunity today, right now, to enact this powerful divine kiss. We know what is being asked of us. We know what we need to do. We may struggle to live out this grand invitation. But God has already placed all we need inside each of us. This world is attainable when and if we say yes to God and act accordingly. So, let us say yes to God again today and take up the work of living mercifully, in truth, and acting with righteousness and peace.

Going Deeper

How do you live out these four promises of mercy, truth, righteousness, and peace? Have you experienced a divine convergence of them in your life?

Saturday

Righteousness shall go before him,
and peace shall be a pathway for his feet.

PSALM 85:13

In life, our paths include the places we hope to go, the places we end up not going, and the places we are forced to go because of circumstances. This is life's journey, with both its challenges and joys. However, the psalmist is clear about these pathways, where they will lead, and how we get there. Righteousness shall go before us, and peace shall be a pathway for our feet.

We are all faced with pathways in our lives—choices we must make. Walking through life, we are urged to pay attention to what and who is around us. We are asked to see them and the world through a lens of justice and righteousness, balancing out the mountains and valleys. As we move along these paths, God calls us to respect the dignity of every human being, regardless of our many differences, and to be merciful when we encounter truths. We are advised to listen to God and to seek out God's voice amidst the noise of life. We are reminded to honor and praise God always, standing in awe of God's majesty and power and all-knowing wisdom and presence in our lives. We are rescued by God's faithfulness and salvation even when we don't see a way forward. We are guided to turn our hearts and minds toward God, especially when overwhelmed with fear, sorrow, or grief. We remain open to partnering with God, being God's hands and feet in the world. All this, so we can enjoy the fruit of peace.

In my book *Becoming Who I Am*, I wrote a meditation about directions. I share part of it with you as we go forward into Advent. May it be a blessing on this journey and give you hope for the life to come.

When going forward in life, it may seem overwhelming and unpredictable, resembling more of a winding road with many twists and turns. But looking backward, it always seems like a straight line; it makes sense! I was meant to be in those places at those times. Knowing that God has a purpose for my life (Jeremiah 29:11) keeps me grounded. Knowing that each experience, whether difficult or filled with joy, is an opportunity to learn from and listen to God, gives me confidence, courage, and peace. Remember forwards. Believe backward.

Going Deeper

Spend time with the last words of the meditation: Remember forwards. Believe backward. What does that mean to you? How might this approach impact your journey of faith?

The Third Week of Advent

Sunday

Happy are they who have the God of Jacob for their help! whose hope is in the LORD their God; Who made heaven and earth, the seas, and all that is in them; who keeps his promise for ever;

PSALM 146:4-5

As Christmas nears, the world around us enters a frenzy. The anxiety is palpable as everyone rushes to buy the perfect Christmas gift. We mean to show our love through these gifts, but I often wonder: Can a beautifully wrapped gift underneath the Christmas tree truly show love? Can love be placed in a box, wrapped up, and put on hold until it's time for the gifts to be opened? When did love become so commercial and transactional? Have we lost the meaning of real love?

In scripture, we encounter four types of love: *philia*, a love of friendship and affection shared by equals; *storge*, a love within familial relationships; *eros*, a love of passion and attraction; and *agape*, a love that is unconditional, selfless, and sacrificial.

Agape is the love shown by God for God's people in the incarnation. It is the love represented in a little babe who is to be born not in a palace filled with riches and power but in a stable surrounded by humble field workers and visited by foreigners seeking a king who would transform the world. This love is almost indescribable. One could argue that we can know true joy because of that love, the love of God that dwells in and among us.

This love is impossible to wrap and place under the Christmas tree, for it is a love that must move and be lived. It is a love given freely by God, who has from the moment of creation kept God's promises. In Advent, we are invited to stop with the busyness of life and delight in God's love and in God's promises of liberation and salvation. Instead of rushing through the season, let us, like expectant mothers, rejoice in the expectation of new life! Let us commit to the joy of knowing we are loved by God who created us in

God's image and who, despite our brokenness, never abandons us, a God whose promises are forever.

Oh, what joy it is to know that type of love! Let us always anchor our hope in God's love, and may we, in this Advent season, prepare not the Christmas tree but instead prepare our minds, hearts, and spirits to receive the hope, love, and joy that only God can provide.

Going Deeper

Think about how you will give the gift of love this season—not wrapped in bows and paper—but through kindness, selflessness, and generosity.

This Week's Author

Nancy Frausto is the director of Latinx studies at the Seminary of the Southwest. She is the first and only DACA (Deferred Action for Childhood Arrivals) beneficiary priest in the Episcopal Church and was a founding member of the Diocese of Los Angeles Sanctuary Task Force.

Monday

*Who gives justice to those who are oppressed,
and food to those who hunger. The LORD sets
the prisoners free; the LORD opens the eyes of the
blind; the LORD lifts up those who are bowed
down; The LORD loves the righteous; the LORD
cares for the stranger; he sustains the orphan and
widow, but frustrates the way of the wicked*

PSALM 146:6-8

During my time in seminary, I had the pleasure
of serving my field education year at a historically
African American church, where I learned of their
call-and-response worship style. Some of my favorite
memories serving this church were the moments of
complete joy as the preacher would shout, "God is
good!" and the whole congregation would respond
with, "All the time. God is good!" Is that not the
most beautiful expression of faith? One of the lessons
I treasure the most from serving in that church is the
congregation's unwavering faith in God's goodness,

for even amid oppression, God will show us God's love and mercy.

In reading today's psalm portion, I could picture my sweet congregation praising God and God's goodness, shouting in great joy to the heavens, "God is good! All the time. God is good!" Like that beautiful congregation, how could we not rejoice on this day and every day when our sacred text reminds us of God's love for those that the world rejects, for the unwanted, unnamed, and unappreciated?

In these words from the psalm, we find the faithfulness of God's care for those who hunger. God will bring liberation from all chains that enslave the beloved children of God. God's goodness will be for all people. God has promised to lift the downtrodden, love the righteous, care for the stranger, and sustain the forgotten. No wonder Mary, mother of our Savior, sings a song of resistance that echoes the psalmist's writing, "My soul magnifies the Lord, and my spirit rejoices in God my Savior, for he has looked on the humble estate of his servant. For behold, from now on, all generations will call me blessed; for he who is mighty has done great things for me, and holy is his name." Holy indeed is God's name.

Just as Mary proclaims and as my congregation shouts to the heavens, let us, too, on this day rejoice in the goodness of the Lord! This, my friends, is the good news that our neighbors need to hear. Good news is necessary for survival when the world groans in agony due to the pillaging of resources. Good news must be proclaimed so we might help transform this world filled with anger and fear toward the other, the stranger, and the foreigner into a place of belonging and love. Let us be bearers of the good news by proclaiming that God is good.

As we prepare to celebrate the birth of our Savior, let us experience true joy in the knowledge that our God is a God of goodness who celebrates the wholeness and flourishing of all people.

Going Deeper

In your prayers and in your worship this week, respond with the words, "God is good! All the time. God is good!" You can say them aloud, whisper them, or say them silently to yourself. How does the act of saying these words impact your prayers and worship?

Tuesday

The LORD shall reign for ever, your God,
O Zion, throughout all generations. Hallelujah!

PSALM 146:9

One of my favorite Spanish hymns is "Alabaré,"
written by Manuel José Alonso and José Pagán. This
is a very well-known hymn in Latino congregations,
and it can often be heard as the processional hymn on
Sunday mornings.

Alabaré Alabaré
Alabaré Alabaré
Alabaré a mi Señor

This translates roughly to "I will praise, I will praise,
I will praise my Lord." In my experience, every time
the hymn is sung, parishioners break into joyful
dances; *abuelitas* (grandmothers) and small children
sing the song with their entire bodies. Movements
of praise often go on throughout the song until we
finally arrive at the last stanza, typically with a little

extra perspiration after joyfully and wholeheartedly singing and dancing our praises to God.

The image of the congregation singing "Alabaré" is how I picture the psalmist proclaiming this verse, "The LORD shall reign forever, your God, O Zion, throughout all generations. Hallelujah!" This is a triumphant proclamation for the reign of God, a joyful declaration for the people of God who fix their gaze on God and on the hope that God's kingdom is indeed a place for all. For the early readers of this psalm who knew human frailty all too well, this psalm was a reminder that while the world may be falling apart, there is hope in the reign of God, which will be eternal. This reminder remains the same for us today and is just as important now as it was then.

Too often, we put our trust in worldly things, forgetting that material things, empires, and rulers will fall and come to an end, but God is forever, and with God comes healing, restoration, and liberation! Hallelujah! Praise the Lord, indeed.

May we find time in our day to praise God, dance in the rain, and fill the space around us with shouts of joy, for our God's reign will never end. God's sovereignty fulfills God's promise of justice, righteousness, healing, and peace. In God's love for the world, we receive that light of hope that dispels the shadows of suffering. It breaks down the human-made walls and creates pathways to salvation. As we receive our Lord and Savior, Jesus Christ, this Christmas, we must sing praises to our God.

Alabaré Alabaré
Alabaré Alabaré
Alabaré a mi Señor

Going Deeper

Sing your favorite song of praise. If you can't think of one—or need some inspiration—search for a rendition of "Alabaré." Whether you know Spanish or not, embrace the joy of this praise song.

Wednesday

*When the LORD restored the fortunes of Zion,
then were we like those who dream. Then was
our mouth filled with laughter, and our tongue
with shouts of joy.*

PSALM 126:1-2

Father Greg Boyle, Jesuit priest and founder of a gang intervention program called Homeboy Industries, writes in his book, *Tattoos of the Heart*:

> God is more expansive than every image
> we think rhymes with God. How much
> greater is the God we have than the one
> we think we have? More than anything
> else, the truth of God seems to be about
> a joy that is a foreigner to disappointment
> and disapproval. This joy doesn't know
> what we're talking about when we focus
> on restriction or not measuring up. This
> joy is like a bunch of women lining up in
> the parish hall on your birthday, wanting
> to dance with you.

If you have ever had the pleasure of celebrating your birthday with your faith community, you understand the type of joy that Boyle articulates. It is a unique joy that comes from the love of your fellow siblings who are ready to celebrate you! They are ready to dance with you, for they see your belovedness; they see the image of God in you.

This type of celebration is what we find in Psalm 126. Although it is classified as a community lament, the first two verses are what Mark Throntveit, professor emeritus of the Old Testament at Luther Seminary, describes as "a community song of trust or confidence that skillfully employs metaphor to proclaim God as the one who brings joy out of sorrow, laughter out of tears, and good out of evil." In other words, the first two verses are our invitation to the dance party God has prepared for us. As God restored Zion's fortunes, so has God wiped away the tears and filled the hearts with laughter. And because God has done this before, God can do it again.

Psalm scholar James L. Mays characterizes this psalm as "joy remembered, and joy anticipated." This psalm reminds us that when we call on God, God will show up as God has done in the past. May we never forget the greatness of God that Boyle describes. May we be partakers of God's grace and share the joy with the multitudes who need to know they are loved and worthy of God's forgiveness. God will show up in the unexpected dance partner, the babe in the manger, the homeboy looking for a way out of violence, and even in a psalmist seeking joy amid laments. May our eyes be opened so we can see God inviting us to dance.

Going Deeper

The author uses the metaphor of a dance party that God invites us to join. What metaphors resonate with you as you imagine the joy of God showing up in your life?

Thursday

Then they said among the nations, "The LORD has done great things for them." The LORD has done great things for us, and we are glad indeed.

PSALM 126:3-4

If given the opportunity, would you testify to the great things the Lord has done for you? Psalm 126:3-4 unabashedly testifies to the great things the Lord has done. In recognizing God's goodness, the psalmist exclaims they are filled with joy. As we continue our Advent journey, I invite all of us to take a moment to pause and contemplate how God has and is working in our lives.

The invitation to "stop and smell the roses" may come to mind. Imagine if we stopped to relax, enjoy, and appreciate the beauty that God has placed before us. I ask again: if given the opportunity, would you testify to the great things the Lord has done for you? What things has God done for your family, your community of faith? Where in this time have you experienced God's light guiding you? How has God's love replenished you? Have you known God to be by your side in times of trouble? Has God shown up in a friend, providing a listening ear or a shoulder to cry on? What good things has God done in your life?

In this psalm, we hear about the restoration and rebuilding of the temple in Jerusalem in the sixth century BCE. If God can restore the temple in Jerusalem and those in exile back to a land of their own, then God can do it all.

May the joy of God's faithfulness toward us and the anticipation of God's eternal reign be our hope as we prepare to receive Christ in our hearts this Christmas. As the psalmist does, let us not be ashamed to testify on the works of God in our lives. In whatever way we can attest to God's goodness, let us shout it from the mountaintop. Let our testimony of faith be heard all over the nations so those who live in shadows of doubt may be witness to the light that God can and will always provide for those who choose to follow in God's way.

Going Deeper

Take a moment to write a testimony of the good things God has done for you. Recall the moments of healing, restoration, and provision. As you reflect, may your heart be filled with gratitude and joy for the tangible evidence of God's love in your life.

Friday

Restore our fortunes, O LORD, like the
watercourses of the Negev. Those who sowed with
tears will reap with songs of joy.

PSALM 126:5-6

When we think about Advent, we often think of
the season as a time of preparation and anticipation.
Today, I would like us to think of Advent as a time of
longing: a longing for a Savior to be born, a longing
for the suffering of the world to end, a longing for
the living water that will quench our thirst. Imagine
a longing, as the psalm says, that will restore our
fortunes like the watercourses of the Negev.

Picture the desolate desert lands of the Negev. Such
desert lands may show no sign of life, but the faithful
call out to the Lord to restore the watercourses and
transform an empty desert into gardens filled with
new life. As we move closer to Christ's birth, our souls
long for renewal. We long for a transformation that
will turn the barren landscapes of our souls into plush

evergreen gardens. Just like the psalmist pleads with God for a transformation, we, too, plead for God to transform our empty lives and fill them with God's love and grace. As the psalmist writes, we plead for our tears to transform into songs of joy.

The longing and anticipation of the Advent season give us an opportunity to interrogate the parched places of our personal and communal lives. In this time, we can surrender our brokenness, tears, and disappointments so that we can be transformed. This transformation will not save us from further suffering, but it will strengthen us in the knowledge that God will always take what is barren and empty and mold it into something new.

It amazes me to think of all the beautiful things God has done for humanity. Our sacred scripture is filled with love letters from God, who always tries to reach us, no matter how often humanity fails. God is always ready to transform, always waiting for us to turn back to God.

The birth of our Savior is the ultimate example of God calling us back, an offering of self so that we may know a new way of life. The incarnation is God's most intimate love letter to us. God in human form is the one sign we cannot ignore. We know that God has come to restore, renew, and transform because that is Jesus's ministry. His life and teachings are God's invitation for transformation. Jesus is the roaring waters of justice, hope, and love. Jesus is the living water that will soothe our parched spirits. Jesus is our salvation. We long for his second coming and pray that the songs of joy will never cease.

Going Deeper

Set aside some quiet time today. Allow your mind and heart to explore the question: what is your deepest longing? Then consider how God might answer (or may already have answered) that longing.

Saturday

Those who go out weeping, carrying the seed, will come again with joy, shouldering their sheaves.

PSALM 126:7

I have never been much of a gardener; as a matter of fact, every time I have tried to keep a plant, it withers away. This is quite frustrating as my mother has the most beautiful gardens. She tends to them with so much care and devotion. As spring nears, the fragrant smell of flowers surrounds our home. My mother truly has a gift. Every seed she plants grows and flourishes under her care. I once asked her what her secret was, and she said, "I give them my all; my time spent caring for my garden is my prayer time, my time to thank God for my blessing, and even my time to weep. My garden holds my prayers, my secrets, my tears."

Reading today's selection of the psalm, I could not help but think of my mother. In times of turmoil, she has remained faithful to her belief that God will restore, provide, and lift her up. The tears that soak the soil in her garden nourish the seeds of her faith, providing her strength and resilience in times of trouble. Except for my grandmother, I do not think I have met a more faithful person than my mother, for even her tears are offered to God so that God may create a new life with them.

The last verse of Psalm 126 assures us that our tears are not in vain. This comforts me as I think about the many tears spilled over the injustice and brokenness of our world. These tears are not invisible; God sees our tears and our struggles and journeys with us as we strive to live a better life each day. Our tears will dry, and we will come again with joy.

This Advent season, let us take care of our spirits as if they were gardens filled with the most beautiful and exotic flowers. May we tend them with the same love and dedication my mother tends to her garden. May we prepare the soil to plant seeds of hope that will grow and sustain us as we wait for the arrival of our Savior, for it is in the birth of Christ that we will know true joy because our Savior has come into the world to show us a new way of life.

Going Deeper

Have you ever considered your tears as a water that nourishes and nurtures your faith? The next time you cry—maybe even today—think of these tears as another gift of God and as an offering back to God.

The Fourth Week of Advent

Sunday

The earth is the LORD's and all that is in it,
the world and all who dwell therein.

PSALM 24:1

In my Hebrew class in seminary, my professor pointed out that the phrase "have dominion over" is best translated as "serve and preserve." I like this reframing, as it is a paradigm shift from oppressive power and control to loving, tending, and stewarding.

I am proud to belong to a denomination that considers climate change a scientific fact. I am proud to belong to a church that recognizes the need for confession and reconciliation and action, not just for sins (seeking our own will, not our Creator's will) against God and other humans but also for our failure to serve and preserve all of creation: land, water, and our non-human relatives.

In Native culture, there is the idea of considering the impact a decision has on seven generations—and if we act out of love, having been created in the image of our loving Creator, then we will remember that the earth is indeed the Lord's and all that is in it. We are called to care for the earth and treat its resources not as commodities but as gifts. Our daily choices either reflect our love for God's creation or not.

I serve in North Dakota, a land of stark and (in the winter) deadly beauty. It is also a land of oilfields, and on my way to work, I drive past flares of methane, an eerie sight, especially at night. I am aware that I live, as we all do, on stolen Native land that was cared for by Indigenous Peoples for thousands of years before colonization. In this context, I strive to live in harmony with other people, with myself, and with "this fragile earth, our island home," as we say in one of our prayers.

As we observe Advent, many of us have wreaths at church and at home. My son always enjoyed helping gather greenery for our home Advent wreath. We would talk about the different trees, usually pine, cedar, and holly, that we used. Cedar is a medicine tree in Cherokee tradition, in Arikara, the tribe I married into, and in other tribes as well. Plants traditionally are seen as helpers to humans. When we honor the earth and all that is in it, we honor our Creator.

Going Deeper

This Advent, reflect on how your actions, individually and collectively, can embody your love of Creator and creation.

This Week's Author

Kim Fox serves as the missioner for reconciliation, creation care, and congregational ministry development for the Diocese of North Dakota and priest-in-charge for three congregations, two Native and one Anglo. She has also served as a rector and as a hospice, ICU, and level 1 trauma chaplain.

Monday

*For it is he who founded it upon the seas
and made it firm upon the rivers of the deep.*

PSALM 24:2

Our Creator, who made us in their (Trinitarian) image, also created the seas and the rivers of the deep. This water imagery invokes the water of baptism. Early Christians (and some Christians today) practiced full immersion baptism, sometimes outdoors.

I grew up in North Carolina and spent a good deal of time as a child playing in the creek outside my grandparents' farmhouse. The creek was from an underground spring. A short drive away was the New River. It wasn't a very deep river, but one time when my son was a child, our canoe tipped over (much to the amusement of other family members watching), and we were suddenly in a deep pocket of water. I had put a lifejacket on him but had neglected to wear one myself since it was known to be a shallow stretch of river. Not that day. The more my son clung to me, the more I felt myself sinking—and yet I would have done anything to keep him above water. We were only in the water for a few minutes, but I'll never forget that feeling of panic as I knew that I had to keep him safe despite my fear. I imagine that is how our Creator feels about us: loving us so much and wanting to save us from whatever situation we've gotten ourselves into. Years later, when my son was in college, we returned to the same river on a day of severe flooding and decided against going on the water, as it ran too fast and under the surface were limbs and rocks. We stood safely on the bank and respected the river's raging.

Water is a sacred source. Seas and rivers are living entities, providers of sustenance, both physical and spiritual, yet water levels are rising to dangerous levels due to the human impact on our climate. We see more destructive flooding and other natural disasters and may be tempted to think this is a punishment from God, but we are experiencing the consequences of our failing to love and protect the world and its waters. Sin is when we seek our own will, not God's will. When we remember that our loving Creator made not only humans but also the seas and deep rivers, we might then do better at expressing our love for the waters that sustain us.

When I started studying the Cherokee language, I felt like I was drowning in new information. We were not allowed to speak English, even on lunch breaks, and it turns out I kept ordering a glass of salt instead of water until I was gently corrected by my teacher, who explained that it was the same word with a different tone. Sometimes we need someone to correct us in a loving, not shaming, manner. Fortunately, we have been given guidelines to live in harmony and balance when Jesus gave us the summary of the law, a guide for living lovingly, just as we are loved.

Going Deeper

Think of the different relationships you have with water: baptism, drinking, bathing, swimming, and so forth. How might we be better stewards of the gift of water?

Tuesday

Who can ascend the hill of the LORD?
and who can stand in his holy place?"

Those who have clean hands and a pure heart,
who have not pledged themselves to falsehood,
nor sworn by what is a fraud.

They shall receive a blessing from the LORD.

PSALM 24:3–5A

I attended a seminary that had the affectionate and sometimes ironic nickname, the Holy Hill. I grew up in the mountains, and to this day that is where I feel most at home. My husband and I recently returned from our honeymoon in the Black Hills of South Dakota, where we drove up to Spearfish Canyon one morning and saw waterfalls either frozen solid or running under ice. Surrounded by the cathedral of creation, we stood in wonder at trout fighting against the current and in awe at jutting spires of rock even older than the Grand Canyon. The green of spruce high in the sunlight bestowed a blessing. It was a holy place because God was there with us.

Show Me Your Ways, O Lord

My husband is a tribal ceremonial leader; I am a priest and poet. But are my hands clean and my heart pure? Most assuredly not. That is not because I don't want to be clean and pure, but I must confess the ways I've fallen short, the things done and left undone. This is why I like the collect for purity:

> Almighty God, to you all hearts
> are open, all desires known, and
> from you no secrets are hid: Cleanse
> the thoughts of our hearts by the
> inspiration of your Holy Spirit,
> that we may perfectly love you, and
> worthily magnify your holy Name;
> through Christ our Lord. *Amen.*

We know we often miss the mark, but we ask for God's help in coming clean and when we know better, to do better. In striving to live in right relationship with God, neighbor, and ourselves, we are committing ourselves to show love and gratitude for all the blessings we've been given.

We all want blessing. But we don't earn blessing. Like grace, it is freely given and sometimes out of the worst circumstances can come new life or at least new understanding. Prosperity Gospel preaches that if we're right with God, we'll receive material blessing, a convenient theology for the rich to stay rich and even get richer. But I believe in original blessing, when our Creator saw that it all was good. When we turn our back on those blessings, we must ask forgiveness and seek reconciliation—with God, neighbor, and with our own vulnerable and sometimes tragic selves.

Going Deeper

Name aloud (or write down) things you have done—and left undone—that have fallen short of the desire of God. Then offer those actions to God in prayer, closing with the words of the collect for purity.

Wednesday

*Such is the generation of those who seek him,
of those who seek your face, O God of Jacob.*

PSALM 24:6

As I type these words, it has been more than a
year since I saw my son's face in person. He had an
unfortunate bout with Covid-19 when I planned
to visit him over the summer. To say we were both
disappointed is a gross understatement.

Of course, we have texted and talked and sent
pictures, but that's not the same as seeing each other
face to face. We know this about our loved ones. But
do we remember the same sentiment when it comes to
our relationship with God? Of course, scripture tells
us that it was a perilous thing to look at the face of
God. It just wasn't done. That is, not until the birth of
Jesus, and the face of an infant and the sound of his
cries filled a stable in Bethlehem.

I have a week left in Advent before I can claim
another year of "getting through" Christmas. For us

priest types—and non-priests, too!—it can sometimes seem like Christmas can't be over fast enough so that after the last service, we can finally collapse. This past Christmas Eve, I drove six hours roundtrip to three different towns for worship services. I jokingly say I'll be "dead" by Christmas Day—and hope that I'll be able to find some time to rest and recover.

In Revelation, we are assured we will one day see God face to face and not as a stranger. But with the incarnation—with Jesus's birth—we can see God-in-Christ face-to-face. And we have the invitation to seek and see God in the face of others—of those we serve and love as well as in the faces of strangers and enemies.

There are just a few days left of Advent. Surly preacher that I am, I can still decide to enter fully into Advent and seek not only God's face but also God's will in my life. What shall I do? How shall I serve? Only with God's help. And God's never-failing love.

Going Deeper

Look in the mirror and see God face-to-face in the reflection. Be intentional this week to look with new eyes at those around you, seeking God in all those you encounter.

Thursday

Lift up your heads, O gates;
lift them high, O everlasting doors;
and the King of glory shall come in.

PSALM 24:7

Trigger warning: this meditation deals with abuse.

In the 1980s, when my dad was serving at now-closed Bitburg Air Base in Germany, we often passed through the security gate and a sign that depicted the level of threat or alert. Years later, when I first went to meet someone here at North Dakota's Minot Air Base, I neglected to stop at the visitors' center, somehow on autopilot, thinking I could just drive up, have my car saluted for being an officer's vehicle, and drive through. That is not what happened. I was directed to return to the visitors' center to have my photo taken, a form with my sponsor's name prepared, and my background checked as I waited. Only then could I get through the gate.

Another time, I went to the Blue Christmas service on base; at a priest, I had offered this service in congregations in acknowledgement that sometimes the holidays can be hard and not always cheerful and bright. The chapel was the very same military-issue design as at Bitsburg Air Base, where, as a high school student, I was sexually abused by an adult I had trusted.

Upon entering the gate on base in North Dakota that snowy night right before Christmas, the memories of the abuse came flooding back to me, and I was overcome with emotion. The chaplain at the Blue Christmas service, also an Episcopal priest, offered prayers for healing, and that comforting ritual opened the way for a more peaceful Christmas for me.

Many of us have suffered abuse, whether sexual, verbal, physical, or emotional, and sometimes all of the above. I know firsthand how these experiences can cause us to put up gates for self-protection, but the peace that passes all understanding is always open to us. This doesn't mean that it will always be easy to allow ourselves to experience the comfort of God's presence, but if we allow the King of Glory to come in, we can know that God never desires hurt or injury or tragedy of any kind. We may or may not be able to forgive our abusers, but we can focus on ourselves and on our own healing, with God's help.

Admittedly, I don't like the colonial connotations of the word "King," but I like the idea of glory, of pure and unadulterated joy that comes from any small measure of healing until the day when there is no more suffering or sighing and when God shall wipe away every tear.

Going Deeper

Do you have a painful experience for which you need healing? Research to see if there's a Blue Christmas service offered near to you. You might also reach out to a clergy person or counselor for prayers for healing.

Friday

Your love, O LORD, for ever will I sing.

PSALM 89:1A

When I was a young girl, I sang in the choir, not
because I wanted to, but it was the only way I could
get close to the altar since girls couldn't be acolytes.
Now I'm a priest. See how well it works to censor the
Holy Spirit?

As choir members, we wore red cassocks and white
cottas. We used bobby pins to secure our beanies
on our heads. I remember fits of giggles when we
sang, "Come let us worship and fall down," and
the clanging echo when a boy acolyte dropped the
processional cross on the cold stone floor.

These days, I preside at the altar. But I sometimes
look out and imagine myself as a little girl in the choir
stall, longing to be up at the altar where the men were,
where the boys were, where the action was. I do not
chant the eucharistic prayers. My voice is not strong

or good enough. Yet I still sing inwardly. I sing in my soul when I invite people to "lift up your hearts."

I pray this Advent that you do some singing, inner or outer, and that you know your offering is dear to the Lord, whose angels and archangels sing with us. I pray for war to cease and suffering to be reprieved. I pray for peaceful deaths. I pray we recognize life when we live it. I pray we have the humility to receive love and the assurance to know we are beloved by our Beloved. And of God's love, forever will I sing.

Going Deeper

Do you sing aloud with gusto or mouth the words? Either way—and through all the possibilities in between—let the songs on your lips be of praise and thanksgiving for God's love.

Saturday

I have made a covenant with my chosen one.

PSALM 89:3A

How we long to be chosen: for promotions and elite programs of study; for recognition by our bosses and by our spouses. Yet this verse from Psalm 89 and the words of our Baptismal Covenant remind us that God has chosen us not for what we have done but for who we are. In baptism, Christ lives in us; we are chosen as vessels for God to work through us.

I tear up every single time I have the honor of baptizing someone, whether infant or elder. It is a thin space where water is water now, but also the water of our ancestors in faith:

> We thank you, Almighty God, for the
> gift of water. Over it the Holy Spirit
> moved in the beginning of creation.
> Through it you led the children of
> Israel out of their bondage in Egypt
> into the land of promise. In it your

Son Jesus received the baptism of John
and was anointed by the Holy Spirit
as the Messiah, the Christ, to lead us,
through his death and resurrection,
from the bondage of sin into
everlasting life. We thank you, Father,
for the water of Baptism. In it we are
buried with Christ in his death. By it
we share in his resurrection. Through
it we are reborn by the Holy Spirit.

This covenant empowers us, by virtue of the Holy
Spirit, to stand up to racism and ageism and sexism
and any other form of prejudice that fails to honor the
dignity of every person. This covenant encourages us
to continue in the apostles' teaching and fellowship.
It commits us to ongoing spiritual growth, not just
through our own merits but through the grace and
consolation of the Holy Spirit.

Soon we will light the Christ candle. Soon it will
be Christmas, but not yet. For today, we are chosen
to be Christ's hands and feet in the world, bringing
light to the dark places of injustice and oppression.
We are chosen to work to bring about a more just and
equitable world. So, go. Go in peace. Go in peace to
love. Go in peace to serve.

Going Deeper

Knowing that you are chosen and beloved of God, how will you serve God and others in your family, church, community, and world?

Appendix

Sunday Psalm Readings
for the Season of Advent

WEEK 1

Psalm 122 *Lætatus sum*

(Year A)

1 I was glad when they said to me, *
   "Let us go to the house of the LORD."

2 Now our feet are standing *
   within your gates, O Jerusalem.

3 Jerusalem is built as a city *
   that is at unity with itself;

4 To which the tribes go up,
   the tribes of the LORD, *
       the assembly of Israel,
       to praise the Name of the LORD.

5 For there are the thrones of judgment, *
   the thrones of the house of David.

6 Pray for the peace of Jerusalem: *
   "May they prosper who love you.

7 Peace be within your walls *
   and quietness within your towers.

8 For my brethren and companions' sake, *
    I pray for your prosperity.

9 Because of the house of the LORD our God, *
    I will seek to do you good."

Psalm 80:1-7,16-18 *Qui regis Israel*

(Year B)

1 Hear, O Shepherd of Israel, leading Joseph
   like a flock; *
       shine forth, you that are enthroned upon the
       cherubim.

2 In the presence of Ephraim, Benjamin, and
   Manasseh, *
       stir up your strength and come to help us.

3 Restore us, O God of hosts; *
   show the light of your countenance, and we
   shall be saved.

4 O LORD God of hosts, *
   how long will you be angered
   despite the prayers of your people?

5 You have fed them with the bread of tears; *
     you have given them bowls of tears to drink.

6 You have made us the derision of our neighbors, *
     and our enemies laugh us to scorn.

7 Restore us, O God of hosts; *
     show the light of your countenance, and we
     shall be saved.

16 Let your hand be upon the man of your
   right hand, *
     the son of man you have made so strong for
     yourself.

17 And so will we never turn away from you; *
     give us life, that we may call upon your Name.

18 Restore us, O Lord God of hosts; *
     show the light of your countenance, and we
     shall be saved.

Psalm 25:1-9 *Ad te, Domine, levavi*

(Year C)

1 To you, O LORD, I lift up my soul;
    my God, I put my trust in you; *
        let me not be humiliated,
        nor let my enemies triumph over me.

2 Let none who look to you be put to shame; *
        let the treacherous be disappointed in their
            schemes.

3 Show me your ways, O LORD, *
        and teach me your paths.

4 Lead me in your truth and teach me, *
        for you are the God of my salvation;
        in you have I trusted all the day long.

5 Remember, O LORD, your compassion and love, *
        for they are from everlasting.

6 Remember not the sins of my youth and my
    transgressions; *
        remember me according to your love
        and for the sake of your goodness, O LORD.

7 Gracious and upright is the LORD; *
    therefore he teaches sinners in his way.

8 He guides the humble in doing right *
    and teaches his way to the lowly.

9 All the paths of the LORD are love and
    faithfulness *
        to those who keep his covenant and his
            testimonies.

Psalm 72:1-7,18-19 *Deus, judicium*

(Year A)

1 Give the King your justice, O God, *
    and your righteousness to the King's son;

2 That he may rule your people righteously *
    and the poor with justice;

3 That the mountains may bring prosperity to the
    people, *
    and the little hills bring righteousness.

4 He shall defend the needy among the people; *
    he shall rescue the poor and crush the
            oppressor.

5 He shall live as long as the sun and moon endure, *
    from one generation to another.

6 He shall come down like rain upon the
    mown field, *
    like showers that water the earth.

7 In his time shall the righteous flourish; *
    there shall be abundance of peace till the
        moon shall be no more.

18 Blessed be the Lord GOD, the God of Israel, *
    who alone does wondrous deeds!

19 And blessed be his glorious Name for ever! *
    and may all the earth be filled with his glory.
    Amen. Amen.

Psalm 85:1-2, 8-13   *Benedixisti, Domine*

(Year B)

1 You have been gracious to your land, O LORD, *
    you have restored the good fortune of Jacob.

2 You have forgiven the iniquity of your people *
    and blotted out all their sins.

8 I will listen to what the LORD God is saying, *
    for he is speaking peace to his faithful people
    and to those who turn their hearts to him.

9 Truly, his salvation is very near to those who fear him, *

> that his glory may dwell in our land.

10 Mercy and truth have met together; *

> righteousness and peace have kissed each other.

11 Truth shall spring up from the earth, *

> and righteousness shall look down from
>> heaven.

12 The LORD will indeed grant prosperity, *

> and our land will yield its increase.

13 Righteousness shall go before him, *

> and peace shall be a pathway for his feet.

(Year C: Canticles 4 or 16)

Show Me Your Ways, O Lord

Week 3

Psalm 146:4-9

(Year A)

4 Happy are they who have the God of Jacob for
   their help! *
       whose hope is in the Lord their God;

5 Who made heaven and earth, the seas, and all
   that is in them; *
       who keeps his promise for ever;

6 Who gives justice to those who are oppressed, *
       and food to those who hunger.

7 The Lord sets the prisoners free;
   the Lord opens the eyes of the blind; *
       the Lord lifts up those who are bowed down;

8 The Lord loves the righteous;
   the Lord cares for the stranger; *
       he sustains the orphan and widow,
       but frustrates the way of the wicked.

9 The Lord shall reign for ever, *
       your God, O Zion, throughout all generations.
       Hallelujah!

Psalm 126   *In convertendo*

(Year B)

1   When the LORD restored the fortunes of Zion, *
    then were we like those who dream.

2   Then was our mouth filled with laughter, *
    and our tongue with shouts of joy.

3   Then they said among the nations, *
    "The LORD has done great things for them."

4   The LORD has done great things for us, *
    and we are glad indeed.

5   Restore our fortunes, O LORD, *
    like the watercourses of the Negev.

6   Those who sowed with tears *
    will reap with songs of joy.

7   Those who go out weeping, carrying the seed, *
    will come again with joy, shouldering
        their sheaves.

(Year C: Canticle 9)

WEEK 4

Psalm 80:1-7, 16-18

(Year A, printed in Week 1)

Psalm 24:1-7   *Domini est terra*

(Year A)

1 The earth is the LORD's and all that is in it, *
    the world and all who dwell therein.

2 For it is he who founded it upon the seas *
    and made it firm upon the rivers of the deep.

3 "Who can ascend the hill of the LORD? *
    and who can stand in his holy place?"

4 "Those who have clean hands and a pure heart, *
    who have not pledged themselves to falsehood,
    nor sworn by what is a fraud.

5 They shall receive a blessing from the LORD *
    and a just reward from the God of
        their salvation."

6 Such is the generation of those who seek him, *
    of those who seek your face, O God of Jacob.

7 Lift up your heads, O gates;
   lift them high, O everlasting doors; *
      and the King of glory shall come in.

Psalm 89:1-4, 19-26 *Misericordias Domini*

(Year B)

1 Your love, O LORD, for ever will I sing; *
   from age to age my mouth will proclaim
         your faithfulness.

2 For I am persuaded that your love is established
   for ever; *
   you have set your faithfulness firmly in the
   heavens.

3 "I have made a covenant with my chosen one; *
   I have sworn an oath to David my servant:

4 'I will establish your line for ever, *
   and preserve your throne for all generations.'"

19 You spoke once in a vision and said to your
   faithful people: *
   "I have set the crown upon a warrior
   and have exalted one chosen out of the people.

20 I have found David my servant; *
    with my holy oil have I anointed him.

21 My hand will hold him fast *
    and my arm will make him strong.

22 No enemy shall deceive him, *
    nor any wicked man bring him down.

23 I will crush his foes before him *
    and strike down those who hate him.

24 My faithfulness and love shall be with him, *
    and he shall be victorious through my Name.

25 I shall make his dominion extend *
    from the Great Sea to the River.

26 He will say to me, 'You are my Father, *
    my God, and the rock of my salvation.'"

Psalm 80:1-7

(Year C, printed in Week 1)

About the Authors

Week 1

Kathryn Nishibayashi is a lifelong Episcopalian. She is the fourth generation of her family to be a member at St. Mary's Episcopal Church in Los Angeles, a church founded for Japanese immigrants but now home to a multicultural congregation. She has held various leadership positions at the parish, diocesan, and churchwide levels. She received her master of divinity degree from Church Divinity School of the Pacific in 2023 and is in discernment for Holy Orders. Prior to seminary, she spent 12 years as an elementary school teacher.

When not busy with church activities, Kathryn enjoys reading, singing, and watching baseball.

Week 2

Atlanta-based speaker and author **Beth-Sarah Wright** works nationwide, encouraging individuals, communities, and institutions to develop the capacity for change and transformation. Beth-Sarah is a former college professor at NYU and Spelman College; she currently serves as the director of enrollment management at Holy Innocents' Episcopal School in Atlanta and an adjunct assistant professor in the department of psychiatry at Emory School of Medicine. She holds a Ph.D. in Performance Studies from New York University, an MPhil in Anthropology from Cambridge University, and a BA (*magna cum laude*) from Princeton University in Sociology and Afro-American studies.

Her body of work addresses the insidious challenges we face in our individual lives, mental health, or communities that require identity shifts and increases in capacities and competencies to bring about sustainable and meaningful change. Beth-Sarah advocates for authenticity in our lives and communities by aligning our aspirational identities with our lived realities.

Week 3

Nancy Frausto, born in Zacatecas, Mexico, immigrated to the U.S. as a child. She is the first and only DACA (Deferred Action for Childhood Arrivals) beneficiary priest in the Episcopal Church and a founding member of the Diocese of Los Angeles Sanctuary Task Force.

A powerful preacher, teacher, and witness to the power of God's liberating love, she is the Diocese of Los Angeles's first Latina leader to have grown up in a Spanish-speaking Episcopal Church who has gone on to pursue ordination. Nancy recognizes the importance of honoring diversity in language, culture, social-economic status, and race in people's stories. Her passion for storytelling and finding God amid chaos, pain, laughter, and joy drives her desire to share her personal story and hear the stories of others who seek, name, and celebrate Jesus's loving presence in their lives.

Nancy is the recipient of the Episcopal Church Foundation and Beatitudes Society Fellowship. She was named one of the "Future 50" Interfaith Leaders in Los Angeles to watch by the Interreligious Council of Southern California. In 2013, Nancy completed her Diploma in Theology from Bloy House, the Episcopal Seminary at Claremont School of Theology; she received the Thomas Cranmer Scholarship for Distinguished Achievement in Liturgical Scholarship and the Preaching Excellence Award. Online magazine relevant.com named her one of their 12 effective Women Preachers. In the spring of 2018, CBS network featured her work on their documentary *Race, Religion & Resistance*.

Week 4

Kim Fox serves as the missioner for reconciliation, creation care, and congregational ministry development for the Diocese of North Dakota and priest-in-charge for two Native and one Anglo congregations. Kim is trained as a racial healing leader and also brings her experience as rector, hospice chaplain, ICU and trauma chaplain, as well as writer and wellness coach to her ministry in North Dakota. She has bachelor's and master's degrees from the University of North Carolina, Chapel Hill, and a master of divinity degree from Virginia Theological Seminary.

Kim serves on the Creation Care, Congregational Development, Convention Planning, and Reconciliation committees as well as serving as secretary for the North Dakota Council on Indian Ministries. Since coming to North Dakota, she has written for Roanridge, United Thank Offering, and North Dakota Episcopal Foundation grants. She was selected to present a workshop at the Episcopal Church's Forma conference. In addition to her own published creative writing, she was a writer for *Forward Day by Day*.

Kim's background is mixed heritage, including Cherokee. She is from the mountains of North Carolina but has come to appreciate the beauty and history of the Northern Plains. She loves being out in nature (preferably when it is above zero!), has learned the art of layering clothes for the weather, and has been thrilled to see bison, moose, and other wildlife since moving to North Dakota.

About the Artist
for the Book Cover

Claudia Smith lives her passions, whether it be with the artist's brush or the writer's pen. As a fine arts graduate from Michigan State University, she shared her love of art with mature young students. She ventured into the commercial  world of art in interior design, mural painting, and freelance art. Publishers found her illustrations and cartooning the perfect match to accompany her writing and that of staff writers. Her oil and mixed-media paintings have been featured in galleries, private collections, and municipal commissions, usually accompanied with her directed poetry. She has been a registered member artist with ECVA (Episcopal Church Visual Arts) for many years.

The painting on the cover of the book is entitled *Windswept Majesty*. It was inspired by a trip to Yellowstone Park and the surrounding area. The painting is part of an ECVA exhibit, "What Are You Seeking? Expectations and Epiphany."

About Forward Movement

Forward Movement inspires disciples and empowers evangelists. We live out our call as a discipleship ministry by publishing daily reflections and online resources. People around the world read daily devotions through *Forward Day by Day*, which is also available in Spanish (*Adelante Día a Día*) and Braille, online, as a podcast, and as an app for your smartphone.

A ministry of the Episcopal Church since 1935, Forward Movement is a nonprofit organization funded by sales of resources and gifts from generous donors.

Learn more about Forward Movement and our work, at forwardmovement.org or venadelante.org.